THE LITTLE

MOR
ROUTINES

**DISCOVER THE TRANSFORMATIVE POWER
OF 'AWE INSPIRING' MORNINGS**

BY KRYSTIAN SZASTOK

© 2019 Krystian Szastok

Independently published by the author
email: krystian@newtide.agency

ISBN 978-1-67974-171-5

Manufactured in the UK

Contents

About the Author

Krystian Szastok moved to the UK from Poland in 2005 as an expat with no skills or notable education. Since moving at the age of 20, he has built a career in digital marketing, from working in small businesses to leading teams in some of the best digital agencies in the country (Jellyfish is a notable example). Krystian has spoken at conferences internationally, helped with SEO, and led training sessions and workshops for FTSE 250 companies. Over the years, his progression has led him to being a highly sought after independent digital marketing consultant. He has run his consultancy as a digital nomad from countless cities in Asia, Russia, and Europe. while practicing morning routines and personal development daily.

Message from the Author

Who is this book for?

If you're someone who wants to achieve more in your life - this book is for you.

If you're a freelancer or a business owner and you have a lot of daily responsibilities, this book is for you.

If you're in a relationship and want to connect with your partner, or if you're currently single, this is a book for you.

I not only talk about morning routines, but also about how to help you discover your inner calling and add more purpose to your life. These qualities and accomplishments will bring you closer to others in your life, and help you grow new relationships.

Why did I write this book?

I wrote this book because I've been practicing morning routines for over 10 years; I've perfected mine, experimented, researched the topic, and realised a lot of the elements are not covered in the books currently available.

I also had a breakthrough in the 'awe-inspiring mornings' thanks to a video by neuroscientist Beau Lotto, whose research has changed my life. Ever since watching his video, I have implemented its lessons into my morning routine. This tiny adjustment made such a huge impact on mine and many of my friends' lives; it changed my perspective so significantly that I wanted to share it with as many people as possible.

Dedications

To my Mum, for a great upbringing in the face of adversity. To Anastasiia my fiancée, for being supportive and tolerant of my many flaws. To my grandmother Krystyna who passed away this year, leaving a huge gap in my life. To my grandmother and grandfather (Babcia Madzia and Dziadek Bogdan) for helping me through my young years. To Jacek Wisniewski & family for being an example of a great businessman and a man in general. To Michael Tucker, for lifelong mentorship helping me make this book happen. To my J2G family: Alex, Kyle, and Tobiano for being there for me every day and delivering value. To Bruce Cat and Chokae Kaleoka, two great mentors who have helped me through some of the hardest moments in my life. To lifelong friends such as Natalie W, Mateusz R, Henry M, Guy and Simon, Tom C, Lukasz D, and many others.

If not for you, this wouldn't have happened and my life wouldn't be anywhere near as amazing as it is.

Also special thanks to Kelly Randall for editing and proof-reading, it's only thanks to her most sentences here flow and make sense.

If not for you, this wouldn't have happened and my life wouldn't be anywhere near as amazing as it is.

Always and forever in your debt, Krystian.

Chapter 1
Why even bother with morning routines?

Taking charge of the day with morning routines

What do Tim Ferriss, Oprah, Tony Robbins, Richard Branson, and Jennifer Aniston have in common? They all get up early and execute a morning routine.

> *'You either mount the day, or the day will mount you.'* - **Krystian Szastok**

As you have probably heard many times, to help others you have to help yourself first.

If you put yourself first and make sure that you're educated, happy, accomplished, and healthy, you will be in a better position to do the same for your family, friends, and others in your community, whether offline or online.

Prioritise yourself, and by doing this, you prioritise your family. When you secure this morning time for yourself, you build a space to store your projects, the hobbies you never got to do, and habits you wanted to create (such as meditation) that you can never find time for. Suddenly just by waking up a little bit earlier, you prioritise your wants - but in the mid and long term, what you really prioritise is the wellbeing of your family. So, your own wellbeing starts to transfer to others.

Start taking charge of the day by tackling your priorities first, ahead of other people's priorities.

Don't let your emails and text messages overwhelm you with their problems, issues, and goals. Ensure that you utilise this time in the morning before the priorities of others flood the gates of your phone or laptop screen. Having your own time provides you with armour to protect yourself from distractions and makes available a better approach for dealing with the incoming challenges that life will put in front of you every day.

Focus on your goals first thing in the morning, focus on the connection with your family and your higher self, instead of other people's problems or useless social media messages that only give you anxiety.

Here's a little practical exercise for you: Listen to an inspirational speech by Eric Thomas or Martin Luther King - note how you feel.

Then, at another time during the same day, spend 5 minutes brainlessly going through your Facebook feed or your Instagram stories - make a note of how they made you feel.

If you're anything like me, you'll notice that the first activity left you feeling inspired and motivated, ready to commit to being better, while the second one didn't do anything at best, and at worst left you harbouring "I'm not good enough!" feelings.

Just a few benefits of having a set morning routine:

★ You will be consistently happier.

★ You will feel more accomplished.

★ You will be more energetic.

★ You will feel like every day has meaning.

★ You will become closer to yourself and your family.

These are just a few of the benefits you'll gain by setting up a good morning routine.

The more time you invest, the greater the benefits you'll reap. The returns will grow over time, just like with any activity repeated over a long period; the gym, swimming, running, learning. You need to put in the time and effort consistently to reap the benefits. However, from morning routines, I found that you can enjoy the benefits from day 1 - and they only grow from there.

Imagine if you could wake up, get inspired, get some exercise, read, meditate, plan your day, hydrate, have your morning coffee, work on your side projects, and send messages to your loved ones - all before the majority of the world is even awake. I did all this today (as I'm writing this book) by waking up at 4am and just 'doing it'.

You can accomplish these things too, just start waking up 15 minutes earlier than you would usually - take small steps. I used to wake up at 7am for a year, because that felt like my absolute earliest (due to climate I wasn't functioning well, it was way too hot in Asia for me).

Chapter 2
Self discovery through morning routines

Morning routines as a path to finding new meaning

Often we find ourselves starved of time throughout the day. We consistently don't have time to go to the gym, to meditate, we sometimes even 'don't have enough time to drink water'.

Implementing a morning routine can change your whole approach to life. It signals to your higher self that you're ready to take on new challenges. It shows that you're happy to take full responsibility for your life.

And with that change, more changes will come that change is being signalled in how you walk, how you interact with the world, because a person with a solid and consistent morning routine feels different, stands different, thinks different.

Once you start practicing and finding this extra 10-15 minutes every morning, you will feel empowered as you start to take charge of your day. There is no doubt about it.

It's all about turning the ship towards the waves and meeting challenges head on, rather than trying to hide away from them.

Then, when you share your progress in your online group or with your friends and family, they are sure to see subtle and substantial changes in your behaviour and attitude.

The accountability that comes from sharing is nothing to be frowned upon: it instils consistency. It helps us carry on every day of the week. It helps us achieve long term goals which, when we set them, felt so far away. But, with every day effort, your morning routine will become stronger and as you see the results, you will likely, as I did, invest more time into it, start waking up earlier and start executing more while most people are still in bed.

Soon enough you will include things like meditation, exercise, or reading into your morning routine. And from these activities, a better understanding of yourself will emerge and a higher purpose to your everyday life will follow.

You don't have to actively graph mind maps or go to a spiritual retreat to 'find yourself' - you're already here, you just have to tune in and listen. When better to do this than when others are still asleep; on your own time, in your own way, you can connect with yourself and find more meaning and purpose to every day.

All you need to do to start is commit 5-10 minutes every morning in the first instance, and set yourself a mini schedule to follow. Start small, stay consistent.

Morning programming benefits

"If you don't program yourself, life will program you!" - **Les Brown**

I don't know about you, but sometimes I wake up although my mind is still asleep and feeling a bit slow in general.

You may have experienced waking up feeling a bit 'empty', 'blank', or worse, waking up after a bad dream and feeling a bit confused.

Often, when dreaming, we can't distinguish our dreams from reality. When watching sad movies - our brains can't distinguish reality from what's on the screen - hence our emotional response to something shown to us on a 50inch black mirror on a wall.

Our brain is in part similar to a computer, much like a machine fine-tuned to help us survive in the wild. It has certain properties of which we can take advantage if we were to actively engage with them.

Many people are unaware that you can actively program your brain. Think of acupuncture for quitting smoking. Or hypnosis.

Every morning you have an opportunity to load up 'a

program' into your brain. Much like how we used to insert CDs into computers or music players.

Every morning you can remind yourself what your values are and connect with them, ensuring that you start the morning from that point of view. By engaging with your values, thoughts about your loved ones, and the responsibilities that give meaning to your life, you can start each day from a stance of courage and openness.

What's the alternative? Sometimes we wake up, we open an email with bad news about our project and we start to feel like failures.

The brain is most susceptible to stimuli just after waking up, so take advantage of it!

Here's what you can do to benefit from this fact:

Write down a few things you care about in life - your goals, desires or values.

Write down why you're important to your family and how much you love them.

Write down a few moments where you felt empowered in the past, on top of the world.

These can be just bullet points, no need to write an essay.

In the morning, if you're feeling you've woken up a bit blank, disconnected, confused - look at this text, ideally on a piece of paper, and really 'feel' these statements and desires. When you read about your goals, visualise them;

when you think about your family, imagine being with them; when you reminisce about moments of power, really remember the details about how and when they happened and why you felt empowered.

This only takes a few minutes, but this will fire up your brain and reconnect you with what's important every morning. By doing this, you can start your day on the right foot. From the outset, you aim towards striving for what's important in life, towards your key goals. Rather than just reacting to whatever happens each day.

My morning routine transformation

I was 20 years old when I left my cosy life in Poland. Studying Economics, living with my Mum, it was a safe life but risked being on a path to becoming mediocre.

After a string of temp jobs, with motivation from my one-time landlord and long-time friend since, Michael Tucker, I managed to get a full-time job in a new hobby I had, web design.

Through the following years, I started to specialise in Search Engine Optimisation and moved towards agency life.

I excelled in this career, I was fully in on the rat race, forevermore excited, yet slowly discovering that something was missing.

Who'd have thought I'd get so far in my life. I had a real career, I was managing a team around me - this was quite an accomplishment compared to the standards of my old life. It was more than I ever dreamt of achieving and more than people from my neighbourhood in Warsaw, where I grew up, would've dreamt of.

I had a great career. There were clear signs that I was going to be successful and I was successful. I was fully committed and loved what I was doing, but still, something was amiss.

From about the age of 15, I regularly read self-improvement books, which developed to reading and practicing meditation, self-improvement willpower practices, and more. I also read a ton online - I'm talking about when Steve Pavlina was in his 30s and had a world-leading website that ranked no.1 for all self-development queries on search engines!

Yet in my career, the harder I ran in the rat race, the more it was revealed, every day, that something was missing. Despite practicing meditation and discipline training, I still often found myself stressed, tense, and sometimes even mean to co-workers, and I felt bad about it.

It took me years, with the help of Chris Winfield's blog back in the day, to come up with the first iteration of my daily routine: the morning gratitude list.

It was a game-changer; something about listing the things I was grateful for every morning helped me get set for the day and be my 'better self'.

Yet it was years until I found the next big breakthrough,

the one that enabled me to become a 5x better me (sorry, Grant Cardone, can't say I'm yet at 10x, but I'm trying!), and perform 5x better every day.

I moved to working remotely, for myself, as an independent consultant. I met my fiancée and we travelled the world, then I made the leap to becoming a digital nomad and finally, after a year of that, I had the next breakthrough and changed things around again.

Let me just pause here and say, I didn't change what's deep inside of me, I am not a different person now. I just project myself onto the world and I react to it better.

How have I accomplished this?

By adding 'awe-inspiring' moments to my morning routine.

This was the missing piece of the puzzle in the morning routine I was using and improving for years, yet I never stumbled across it.

One day I finally listened to a Ted talk by Beau Lotto: How we experience awe -- and why it matters.[1] I experienced the change on the first day of practicing this; I researched awe in the following days to find out how and why it affected my brain in such a wonderful day.

Through the years, by changing up my morning routines, through times of self-doubt, I always move towards a more organised, happier, and productive life, where I am

---

1 Beau Lotto and Cirque du Soleil: https://www.youtube.com/watch?v=17D5SrgBE6g&t=55s

proud of even the small things I have achieved and I feel more connected to the world.

Chapter 3
Changing your mindset

The easiest way out of mediocrity and getting unstuck

Often in life we face difficult situations which we can't solve or address. It sometimes feels that there is no 'right way' around the dilemma and we have to choose the lesser of two evils.

Have you ever found yourself feeling you haven't accomplished anything at the end of the day? Or that even though you worked all day you feel bad about your day, as if it didn't matter and it was all for nothing?

These are often signs of being stuck in life, where things just don't feel right.

Very often the reason for these feelings can be attributed to our daily 'way of thinking' - our 'stance towards life' or our 'approach to life'.

At the end of the day, only we can decide how we tackle the real life events that we face daily. Yet sometimes we stubbornly continue to do one thing, whilst hoping to see a different result.

You must change your own routine and your own habits, in order to see changes around you. We project our life from the inside out.

> *"We can't solve problems by using the same kind of thinking we used when we created them."* - **Albert Einstein**

So, how do we change our 'kind of thinking'? It all begins with changing our habits, making space for our spiritual growth, or just for more thinking about our lives.

Two studies[2] show that people who meditated over an eight-week period had a striking change in the expression of 172 genes that regulate inflammation, circadian rhythms, and glucose metabolism. And this, in turn, was linked to a meaningful decrease in their blood pressure.

This is just one of the many examples of how meditation can improve your life. Meditation, or 'mind-body practices that elicit the relaxation response', can include anything from yoga, listening to calm music and sitting still, to just mindfully doing the dishes or reading. It has been scientif-ically proven, beyond any doubt, that meditation can help you in your everyday life by setting you up for a day as a more composed and collected you.

---

2   Specific Transcriptome Changes Associated with Blood Pressure Reduction in Hypertensive Patients After Relaxation Response Training: https://www.ncbi.nlm.nih.gov/pubmed/29616846 and Harvard Study: Clearing Your Mind Affects Your Genes And Can Lower Your Blood Pressure: https://www.wbur.org/commonhealth/2018/04/06/harvard-study-relax-genes

Over time, by practicing mindfulness and present mind, you will notice the way you think changes. By finally exploring the hobbies you've been ignoring and by practicing and learning things you've always wanted to, but never had time for, the way you approach your days will change. The way you think will be altered, and you will see yourself in a different light.

You will adjust from saying 'I don't have time for meditation' or 'I don't have time to exercise' - to saying 'I made the time to mediate' and 'through waking up 15 minutes earlier, I made time for an exercise session every morning'.

How to know if you're making excuses or if your perception is real

A close friend of mine was recently struggling with his daily and weekly tasks and commitments. He is a dad of two, has a lovely partner, and runs a medium-sized business, along with being involved in multiple networks. One day he messages me and says things are really busy and he is struggling to organise his time properly, complete all priorities before day's end, basically keep all his plates spinning. He felt so busy he thought it was impossible to start any side projects or spend more time helping others.

Next week we speak again and he says "this week has been hell, I had many setbacks, two of my staff had to leave the business, I'm looking for replacements, I had to get involved hands-on into a lot more stuff in the business, which sucked out all my free time, this has been one of the most difficult weeks of my life." You see - the week before, if someone told him things could be busier, he wouldn't have believed it. A week later - he would pay anything to be where he was previously. He didn't perceive the fact he wasn't really that busy.

Often when we're 'close to our max' we don't even realise how much more can we put in. Maybe you just assume you don't have the time for a morning routine, or, in life, you can't start any new projects or keep up with your routines, hobbies, or passions.

My grandmother (may she rest in peace, one of the smartest if not the smartest woman I ever had the pleasure of being in the presence of) once told me an old story. It was told by a wise man:

There was once this man, a family man, he had a small tent in the desert in which he lived with his five children, wife, and the wife's mother. He couldn't stand all the noise, all the business, the children crying all the time, the old woman telling him what to do and how to do it. He goes to the wise man one day and complains saying ' I can't stand this anymore, I hate this life, this is too much. How do I fix this feeling of no space and business?' The wise man told him: 'buy a goat and pin it by a rope to the middle of the tent'. The man was surprised, but who was he to question the wise man's intelligence. He went and bought a goat, and pinned it in the tent. A week went by and he comes back to the wise man and he says: 'Things are even worse! The goat is pooping everywhere, the tent is a mess, this is a nightmare, what do I do?' The wise man says: 'Get rid of the goat'. After this, the man realised his previous reality was just fine, and just a set of circumstances - now he knew things could be a lot worse.

This is a great lesson: always appreciate your current level of business and, where possible, try to sneak in your passion, interests, side business - whatever it is you want to grow aside from your main lifestyle, into this life. As you never know when the Universe will throw another big challenge your way.

> *"Everybody knows we're just a phone call away from being starkly reminded of the fact of our own mortality'* ... *'to suddenly be thrown out of the normal course of your life and be given a full time job of not dying, or caring for someone that is."* - **Sam Harris**

Chapter 4
Awe: the undervalued success factor

What is Awe?

'[Awe is] the emotion that arises when one encounters something so strikingly vast that it provokes a need to update one's mental schemas'[3].

What can experiencing awe do to/for me?

In their research Melanie Rudd, Kathleen D. Vohs, and Jennifer Aaker say: 'We predicted that people induced to feel awe, relative to those induced to feel other states, would be more willing to volunteer their time, would prefer experiential goods over material ones, and would experience a boost in life satisfaction.'

Wouldn't it be great to start your day by experiencing a boost in life satisfaction? To change the stance we make our decisions from for the day ahead?

---

3   Keltner & Haidt, 2003: https://www.bauer.uh.edu/mrrudd/download/
    AweExpandsTimeAvailability.pdf

Awe: we always pursue experiencing it

We constantly seek awe-inspiring moments. Now, if you think about it, which is one of the most popular sights to see in the States? The Grand Canyon. Countless numbers of us pursue skydiving or climbing/hiking to high altitude spaces or even cityscape viewpoints, from which we can see a great view: they make us feel small, yet connected to the world we live in.

These are just a few examples of us seeking awe-inspiring moments. We just never realised all the benefits, or appreciated that we shouldn't just plan holidays or weekend getaways as stand-alone events, but should plan them and then sprinkle them with some awe-inspiring activities.

How can we experience awe every morning?

For me, the simplest way was to watch wingsuit flying videos while exercising every morning - I always wanted to pursue that passion and I find it amazingly awe-inducing to see people fly, or should I say fall in style?

Many videos online marked as 'people are awesome' present people who overachieve, they make something happen that is unimaginable and unbelievable.

It blows my mind every day and I feel a wave of awe flow over me.

Other examples of morning awe inspiration:

★ Awe-inspiring pictures

★ Quotes

★ Movies

★ Motivational videos

★ Watching the sunrise (something I do nearly every morning)

Getting more 'awe' in your life

Dacher Keltner, in his presentation 'Why Awe Is Such an Important Emotion', says that the average person feels awe two and a half times a week, usually in subtle and surprising ways.

The vast majority of awe experiences come from other people, experiences, and witnessing generosity and wisdom.

As Porter Gale wrote in her book 'Your Network Is Your Net Worth', "The days I don't write or talk to interesting people are the days I'm unhappy" - I've found the same.

If you don't have a network of inspiring people surrounding you, you may not be able to easily walk up to someone everyday and have an amazing, insightful, awe-inspiring conversation. If you were to walk up to random people throughout the day, striking up conversations, and leading a topic to a personal breakthrough, as entertaining as it would be, may give you a certain reputation, not one you may want to get.

However, good alternatives are:

Podcasts
By listening to podcasts such as Secret2Success ('ETthe-hiphoppreacher' YouTube channel), I have upped my game as I realised, these guys are at a completely different level. Listening to them talk with each other about their projects and sharing their ideas on life and relationships consistently gives me awe-inspiring moments.

YouTube channels (like Jordan Peterson's)
This man needs no introduction; his presentations, quotes, and discussions are a constant source of knowledge and, most importantly, wisdom. He has delivered value to me numerous times. Many of his presentations made me go 'Oh my, I finally get it!'. He manages to make seemingly complex psychological or daily routine challenges very clear and easy to grasp.

TED talks
If you're looking for a 10-minute 'awe fix', just listen to a TED talk. Whether it's an official TED event, or TEDx, it doesn't matter, they're all great. You have a huge number of videos there ranging from history, biology, geology, to motivation and overachievers sharing their achievements. I honestly can't remember a time when I watched a TED talk and not walked away feeling inspired, and very often awe-struck.

Motivational quotes

I find simply searching for them on YouTube is great; as so many people create these for the gym, they often have dramatic, inspiring music in the background. They're filled with wisdom for life by great thinkers and, generally, people most of us look up to. Listening to a good motivational quote mix on the way to the gym always improved my output, during any kind of exercise or even a daily work struggle.

Reading books about great people

For a longer time slot, read about great historical figures and their achievements. So many of those dry historical facts come to life when you read about them with an inquiring mind. The kinds of feats that Alexander the Great accomplished (he was called Great for a reason), fearless leaders like Marcus Aurelius or thinkers like Da Vinci are a never-ending source of the calmed kind of awe, delivered slowly by the medium of book pages.

Find your own awe-inducing morning routine hack

Another way of thinking about AWE from Dictionary.com is:

"An overwhelming feeling of reverence, admiration, and fear produced by that which is grand, sublime, extremely powerful, or the like."

I find that some awe-inspiring moments are very personal.

For me, it's the wingsuit videos or amazing tricks/ gymnastics, but it's also motivational speeches by famous world leaders or overachievers.

A nature buff will find amazing nature videos on YouTube awe-inspiring, a stargazer may find videos from the space station particularly inspiring.

For a parent, it may be watching a video of their child realising an amazing achievement, whether it's crawling, taking its first steps, or school performance.

To give you a few other ideas, Datcher Keltner and Jonathan Haidt in their research paper[4] note that the experience of awe may come from:

★ Beautiful people and scenes which produce awe-related experiences that are flavoured with aesthetic pleasure.

★ Perceptions of exceptional ability, talent, and skill which flavour an experience with admiration in which the perceived feels the respect for the other person that is not based on hierarchical dominance or submission.

★ People who display virtues of or strength of character often trigger in other people a state that can be called 'elevation'.

Another method I explored was writing about awe-in-spiring experiences. Or just setting a timer for 5 minutes, closing my eyes and replaying, in my imagination, a past moment of awe. As we all know, our brains often don't

---

4   Keltner and Haidt 2003: https://greatergood.berkeley.edu/dacherkelt-ner/docs/keltner.haidt.awe.2003.pdf

know the difference between our dreams and reality, so this way of inducing awe is achievable anywhere and at any time.

Experiencing awe 'out there'

Ever since discovering the positive effects that awe can have on your brain and your mind, I decided to seek them out as I travel and actively plan one or two potentially awe-inducing moments during trips.

I have found that, over time, my sensitivity to events of awe is increasing. What I mean by that is, the more often I train myself to experience awe, the less it takes to experience it again, which is great, my appreciation for the little things in life is through the roof!

Most of the time, the highest spot in a given city or town will give you an amazing view; I find them very awe-inducing.

Hiking and climbing can take you to very awe-inspiring spots; try to find picturesque routes among hills and mountains.

Chapter 5
Morning Routines

Approaching morning routines positively vs negatively

When we willingly dive into water, the feeling is way better and the process smoother than when we get thrown or fall into it. You've seen the difference between Olympic swimmers diving into the water and a blooper or goofy video of someone being pushed into the water and how they fall into it confused and making a massive splash.

There is a big difference between my past when I was forced to go to school, and myself now; my resistance and negativity flowing from that resistance created a barrier I couldn't overcome. It wasn't that school was bad, or the teachers didn't care - it was simply that I didn't have a choice and I couldn't shape things the way I wanted them to be. I remember thinking 'once I'm done with school I'll never read a book again or never study again, I hate this stuff'. It's vivid still, years later!

If the young me was told 'you will spend the rest of your life reading books every day and studying different disciplines and educating yourself via online courses and even paying for mentors and knowledge' - he would never have believed it. It was totally outside of my possibilities, in my mind at that time, anyway.

But as you grow up, you realise learning is useful, knowing things helps tremendously in life and more importantly, you can choose when, what, and how you learn. I think that creates a huge difference in results and your daily experience.

It's the same with morning routines. Once you embrace waking up earlier, once you wear it like a badge of honour and set yourself targets for morning time and routines, you will start thriving because you're doing it out of your own free will.

When we can see benefits in something and we feel proud of performing a certain activity, we get that boost of self-esteem and we want to share it with others.

I certainly wasn't getting that boost at school, I had to drag myself in and I skipped many classes.

Now when I start to study a new topic, like with Python programming recently, I'm super excited. It's difficult, and I'm bad at it, but I am enjoying the process as I know the end goal and what value it will deliver in mine and my close ones lives.

Start small and build up

I always recommend starting small; pick whatever comfort level you can realistically and consistently achieve.

It's way better to have a 10 minute morning routine that you will do every day, or 5 days out of the week, rather than having an imaginary 1 hour morning routine which you only do three times per week, because often other priorities make you miss most of it or disturb it.

Little things like brushing your teeth and making your bed, as recommended many times in the past, are proven small parts of the routine that help you get started. Adding to those set elements of the day is easier than building whole new habits.

I suggest you start with a small three-step morning routine, then up it to five and so on, until you're happy that your balance of 'getting things done' in the morning vs your daily input and the dreams you want to achieve is established.

Don't eat the frog in the morning - start with an easy win instead

I tried the well-known tactic of eating the frog many times in the past. It was great sometimes - it was very encouraging to tackle the biggest task straight away in the morning.

What I found, though, is that, in some scenarios, it didn't

work for me - so with any of these universal truths or recommendations, you should always try it for yourself and experiment.

For example, sometimes the biggest task isn't the most urgent one. Say I promise a client something that's a small task - an email with a recommendation, I know they need it as soon as possible. But instead, I decide to eat the frog and start my day with a 3-hour research piece for someone else. It's not as time-gated but it is the one task I'm dreading the most for the day.

After those 3 hours, I'm done and pumped for that day, now I'm strong! But my other client, just had to wait 3 hours for a tiny email and now possibly feels neglected or forgotten about - that I dropped the ball.

On some days we wake up a bit tired, it happens to all of us. Sometimes in life, we will have such big challenges that we simply want to just stay in bed, curl up into a ball and disappear from world view. I get that, I've been there, family tragedies certainly fall into that category. On days like these, when I try to tackle the day, every small thing requires a lot more effort. Getting out of bed is a challenge. If I tried to start such a day with that biggest task - I just wouldn't do it. I'd give up and go back to bed; you need to stick to the things you can do.

There is no point approaching a huge task with no energy. That's not how things work. If you have ever watched Strongman competitions, or the modern remake of it that's way more entertaining - CrossFit, you can see that they go at each task with maximum energy and maximum effort on every challenge. You can't lift that huge weight without the required energy; if you tried, you'd just walk up to it and lay on it or lay under it - without energy you can't tackle a big challenge.

What creates energy? It's all within us somewhere, we just have to find it and unlock it.

So instead, I'd start with the smallest, fastest task. I'd sometimes queue up a few of these in a row to get myself on a roll. I'd build on that success. I'd schedule tasks that you are fully in control of.

This is very much what mentors try to draw on when they recommend making your bed or brushing your teeth, it's a similar energy and motivation generator in the mornings.

I now schedule a few small things that make me feel like a winner first thing in the morning. I will not be blocked by some big project that's a real challenge. I will build strength, inspiration, motivation, and belief in myself every morning, by winning. Once I have finished 2-3 things I get up, I stretch, I walk across the room for some water like a boss, because I feel I'm winning because I just 'nailed it'. Endorphins are flowing now and so is the energy to tackle bigger tasks. Still in the morning, maybe within 30 minutes of starting the day, I jump ahead and grab the bull by the horns and, with the correct approach, with the correct energy, I win that fight too. I eat the frog, once I'm ready for it. I set myself up for success.

Warming up for the day

'We don't go to war without a plan' -
Eric Thomas

A boxer warms up before a fight, a footballer warms up before going on the pitch. Yet we just go in to many of our life situations simply hoping to do our best. When realistically, you're going in cold.

A strategist plans a war, every assault, every engagement with an enemy.

I remember working in this business once, and every time we had a meeting I noticed that these guys, the business guys are well prepared. For any meeting! They didn't go into a room with anyone, for any purpose, without being prepped. Making a few notes for arguments, or reviewing the recent facts and the situation for context.

Whereas I was going in cold. I'd say, "I want to ask for a raise, simple, I'll just say 'I want x money please'". They would quickly counter with a challenge, asking what additional value did I bring to justify it, for example. And that's where my plan ended, I didn't have anything prepared, I didn't have a list of things that justified my request. Then more questions followed and I had to wiggle my way through them. The fact was that I was worth way more money than I was earning - and I believe you are too if you feel so and you can justify it. The fact was that I wasn't prepared for any of the potential questions.

Be prepared for things in your life, face them with a plan, don't go into the playing field cold. Using morning routines helps you accomplish just that: being well prepared for the day ahead and facing it being your best self.

The things I don't recommend doing first thing when you wake up

To set yourself up to win each day, right from the outset, it's key to do certain activities and perform your morning routine, but it's also equally important to break a few bad habits and ensure that life's challenges won't be thrown at you before you're ready for them.

Essentially, I try to complete a few things that are fully in my control first thing in the morning, so anything out of my control, or anything I can fail at, I don't do.

For example, I won't risk performing highly technical or difficult tasks that I may fail at. I won't read any emails first thing in the morning because I don't want to feel like a failure if I have bad business news. I won't check my social media in case someone disagrees with me or my number of followers has dropped.

I want to ensure that my day starts positively, so I'll only allow myself positive inputs - whether its positive music, motivational speeches, a good book, or vigorous exercise.

I avoid bad inputs such as:news (via TV or online) - I bypass this pretty much all together unless it may impact me or I can make a difference. For example, economic issues in Venezuela may lead to interesting investment opportunities, or I can donate to help people there. However, once I know it's happening, I don't need updates 5 times a day. Most news I can't do anything about and it sends negative messages to my mind, so why even bother? It's like with a diet - you want to cut out the negative elements as much as possible.

Social media - never check any feed in the morning, often bad news flows through and can catch your attention.

Emails - very rarely they're negative, but why take the risk? I don't even open the mailbox until I've done my morning routine. Okay, in the planning stage of it, I may look at my emails, but I mostly go by my calendar.

Notifications - Text, WhatsApp and Messenger notifications all hold distractions. As I pick up my phone in the morning, I swipe them away for later.

Bad memories - I divert my mind away from them by meditating first thing and creating a sort of mental shield.

How to decide what to put in your morning routine

When putting together my morning routine I chose elements that I felt were missing from my life, the kinds of activities I was neglecting and never making time for.

I also experimented a lot along the way, adding and removing things, questioning each day:

~ How accomplished do I feel after this morning?

~ Throughout the day, was I on edge when working, did I feel tense or stressed?

~ How ready do I feel to take on new challenges?

~ Did this morning help me become a better person?

~ Have I contributed to someone else's life through my morning routine?

~ Was my morning long enough?

~ Do I feel energised?

~ Do I feel connected to the world?

~ Is my body stretched and hydrated?

~ Is my brain switched on and sharp and ready for the day?

There may be things in your life that you keep putting away for later, or 'one day when I do x, then I'll do y'.

You may be wanting to start a side project, but you keep postponing it as you don't have time.

I used to want a 'side hustle' too, but after work I always felt exhausted. I had already worked that day, so why should I continue working into the evenings? I just couldn't fit that side project into my evening routine.

Things changed once I started waking up earlier and I spent 15-30 minutes every morning on the side project. This helped me write, send some emails and, this way, in the afternoons after my 'day job', I'd find myself pulled back in to do a bit more on the side project. This also made the weekends a lot better, as when I started working on my side project on a Saturday morning, it was so much easier to spend extra time on it and finally get it moving.

You may want to make a list of things that you're postponing in life and realistically see what can be fitted into a morning routine.

Many of us meditate or exercise every morning - these are some of the most popular morning routine activities out there as we constantly say we don't have the time for them.

It may be reading a book that you keep putting off - great, start with 5 pages every morning, or even 2 pages. For the rest of the day you'll have this new feeling of 'I did something today I was postponing', and that good feeling will help you in all kinds of situations.

Preparing healthy meals is an activity we sometimes postpone. As you know, diet is 80% of the success when it comes to being and feeling fit, so why not spend time each morning on planning your meals for the day? The most common mistake in trying to keep to a diet is to get 'out there' without any prepared meals or a plan of what you'll eat. This is when you grab a can of coke, crisps, and a sandwich for lunch and makes you feel like you 'lost another day'. Spending the additional time in the morning on planning your meals and preparing something may be the difference between sticking to your diet and having an unplanned cheat day .

Planning and scheduling the day ahead has been a biggie for me. Ever since implementing the calendar where I manage each of my days and all my activities and the work I do, I have found that if I schedule things, and as a result see them coming, I don't get as stressed by them. In fact, by planning the day, I learned to also plan slots of preparation time. Therefore, as the events of the day roll out, as I have client calls or presentations, I always have time to be extra prepared. In the past, I used to schedule my calendar too tightly, which meant coming in 'cold' and that was never a good feeling.

Painting or drawing is another hobby that I used to postpone as there wasn't time. Again, you don't have to set up a studio with special lights, just spend 5-15 minutes drawing in the morning. By spending this time, you unlock your more creative self for the rest of the day by activating the right side of the brain early.

My personal 3 step mini morning routine

Here is my minimal morning routine which I execute before I'm accessible to others:

1. I watch awe-inspiring videos (usually people are awesome) while I do stretching and light bodyweight exercises. This ensures that the areas of my brain responsible (link to resource) for being creative and wanting to meet challenges head-on are activated. This takes about 5-10 minutes, sometimes longer, depending on how my body feels.

2. I plan the day in my diary, I focus on my top priorities for the day, while hydrating and making/drinking coffee.

3. I meditate and make notes of any ideas that come to my mind during meditation, if I'm being disturbed by my thoughts, I make the session a bit longer.

Usually, all of the above takes 10-20 minutes. Sometimes 30 minutes if I spend longer on any given activity.

This is the bare minimum for me these days; this quick morning routine has helped me to massively improve my daily input and feel inspired for the whole day.

Improving your morning routine

Once you've established a morning routine, with time you may want to improve, play with it, or change it up if it feels stale. No one says that you're bound to it for life.

A good morning routine should evolve with life's needs, your current challenges, and circumstances.

Through the day I try to make notes on my morning, what didn't quite fit, or, for example, a conversation during the day may spur you to try something different.

I keep my routine in a few bullet points in my daily journal for as long as it takes for it to stick. Then if I change it, I will rewrite it again, until it settles in.

As Hal Elrod, author of "The Miracle Morning", says,

"Focused, productive successful mornings generate focused, productive, successful days – which inevitably create a successful life."

Over time your morning routine should become more and more focused, really narrowing down to a few things that matter to you, help you progress in life, and have a great day.

It doesn't have to be the most productive ever to begin with, but over time you'll be in control of it and used to it so you'll be immensely productive. That feeling of control will stay with you throughout the day.

Chapter 6
Common morning routine challenges

1. I'm not a morning person

2. Ok, but I really can't wake up much earlier than I do currently

3. Do I have to do a morning routine every day?

4. I don't have the energy

5. I don't have an extra hour every morning to read books

6. I make improvements to my morning routine, but nothing works

1. I'm not a morning person

Can I do an evening routine instead?

No - that doesn't exist. The purpose is to start the day how you mean to go on, to set the pace for the day.

This is not about becoming a morning person or changing yourself. It's about making small adjustments to have a better day. It starts with the morning, the one time of day that you have complete control of.

I used to hate waking up in the morning, I used to hit the snooze button five times in a row or more. When I didn't have a purpose - that's what I did.

However, when life presented me with a challenge, whether in my work or personal life, and I rose to it - I'd wake up way before my alarm.

Was I a morning person after all? Did I discover my inner morning person? I don't know - all I know is that having a huge challenge or target, that I was pursuing and wanting to tackle, made me get up without snoozing and without complaining that it's dark and cold outside.

Set yourself up for success every morning, even in the case that you're not a morning person. You are your no.1 fan, you succeeding is most important, you guessed it, to you! It's you that you wake up every morning. So why not help yourself to wake up early, happy and motivated, with purpose?

---

2. Ok, but I really can't wake up much earlier than I do currently

---

Ok, I get that, we're all in different stages of life with different lifestyles and daily challenges and circumstances.

I am blessed to be in a position where I can get up at 3.30 am, 5 am, or 7 am and it doesn't impact my life (apart from the shorter evenings perhaps).

To begin with, start waking up just 15 minutes earlier than usual Test if you can do that.

Start small with the easiest, simplest habit; start so small you can't talk yourself out of it.

I used to try to jump straight into waking up 1-2 hours earlier than I was at that time. I would wake up and then snooze my alarm after telling myself 'I need that extra hour of sleep'.

If you wake up just 15 minutes earlier, to capture those extra 15 minutes to finally keep a new habit you've been working towards, you can't honestly tell yourself that '15 minutes sleep is going to make a difference and I need it'.

If all you can do is 15 minutes - fine, just maintain that habit. Eventually, you will be transformed by this one early habit and one day, you'll decide 'now I'll do 20 minutes' - because from this new baseline that's only 5 minutes earlier. Then next month you can add another 5 minutes. These individual extra 5 minutes don't make much difference, and you likely have already adjusted your evenings to allow for slightly earlier wakeups.

3. Do I have to do a morning routine every day?

Studies have shown that 'missing one opportunity to perform the behaviour did not materially affect the habit formation process.'[5]

This is amazing! You can lose a day, you can skip one and have a cheat day. Just don't make a habit out of it! I understand that, occasionally, we can't always maintain our routines in life.

At the beginning, I would recommend practicing morning routines on the weekends too. Once the habit settles in, you can take breaks on the weekends and it won't affect your Monday morning routine.

4. I don't have the energy to wake up early

We often underestimate ourselves and how much we're truly capable of. You have unlimited potential inside of you, waiting to be unleashed. Often if I find myself exhausted - waking up in the night and sleeping badly - it's either because I'm stuck in life or my sleeping habits are really bad.

I've included some sleeping tips at the end of this book - if

---

5   (9. Lally P, van Jaarsveld CHM, Potts HWW, Wardle J. How are habits formed: modelling habit formation in the real world. Euro J Soc Psychol. 2010;40:998–1009. [Google Scholar])

you're happy in your life, feeling accomplished every day, feeling like you're contributing to the greater wealth with your daily activities - then the only reason you might feel tired in the morning and not 'have the energy' to wake up 15 minutes earlier, is if your sleeping habits are poor. Your sleeping habits are easy to tackle - largely they're within your control.

If you're a parent and you've been blessed with a young child, frankly, I'm surprised you even have time to read this! So, congratulations on making the time. If you're waking up 5 times or more per night to tend to your child, change it, feed it and do all those amazing things parents of young children experience - then I'm not talking about you here. Your sleeping habits cannot be changed so easily: the main contributing factor standing in the way of a good sleep is your wonderful children with which you've been blessed. I'm not in any way suggesting that children are obstacles in personal development, only someone ready for the challenge should undertake that particular mission.

This falls into the category of special circumstances. However, 90-95% of us can make major adjustments to our daily and evening routines to sleep better. This way, you can have a sound 7or 8 hours of sleep and wake up early, ready to execute your morning routine and make a change in your life.

5. I don't have an extra hour every morning to read books

Sometimes your priorities may start the moment you wake up, no matter how early you wake up. However, most of us can wake up 15 or 30 minutes early and secure this extra time for ourselves.

I used to think that I would never have a full hour every morning just to sit there and read. For some that's not possible, at some points in our lives that's not possible.

Life will bring circumstances and put challenges in front of you to help you grow; you grow through rising to challenges. Your current challenge may be that no matter how hard you try and schedule things and improve your life, nothing seems to change.

6. I make improvements to my morning routine, but nothing works

Have you ever heard of Les' Brown's story of the Chinese bamboo tree? It goes something like this: The Chinese bamboo tree takes 5 years to grow, and when they go through the process of growing it - the people attending the process - they have to take care of it every day, so it breaks through the ground. But once it breaks through the ground, it grows 90 feet tall in only 5 weeks. It wouldn't achieve this growth if at any time the fertilising and care of it had stopped. Without perseverance and hard work, you can't achieve your goals!

Some things take years to take full effect in your life and you're complaining that a few weeks of putting in 15 or 30 minutes a day are not showing proof?

Morning routines were some of the few things to show immediate effect in my life and I will be eternally grateful for discovering them.

Compare this to a medical degree where you need to put in at least 5 years to see any initial results, but then, you're still required to put in 2 more years.[6] Then, if you want to be one of those doctors you've seen on House or ER, real specialists, that may take another 8 years! You can't quit during the first 5 years, because if you don't get that first degree - you can't skip it and move on.

Imagine if someone told you that you need to go to the gym for 5 years, without taking more than 1-2 day breaks (apart from weekends) to see any results? How many people would even attempt it?

That's why we trust doctors. They have shown resolve over many years and it has been assured that they're experts in their field. Becoming a doctor is extremely difficult. One of my friends managed to make this journey all the way through and let me tell you, the guy was more committed than I ever was in my life. I will forever use him in my

---

6   Source: The postgraduate medical education pathway: an international comparison: https://www.ncbi.nlm.nih.gov/pmc/articles/PMC5704606/

mind or in conversations as an example of someone who made a giant leap in his life through commitment.

Don't give up before you see results, keep practicing, keep improving things.

Chapter 7
Sleeping/Waking up hacks

Over the years I often struggled to wake up early. I'd use the snooze button, and we know what that leads to! It leads to feeling uninspired for the rest of the day, not wanting to get up even more, feeling out of energy, and unmotivated.

I have experimented with many ideas, read books, and worked with mentors on things that can make a real, immediate difference to the way you wake up. There are ways to help you get up earlier, without it feeling as horrible as it may sound.

Light alarm

During summer, the sun is your ally in waking up. Our bodies are naturally tuned to wake up with it. Keeping windows, blinds, or shutters open is recommended so that you can use the sun to your advantage.

I found waking up in the winter was the bigger problem because there was no sun. Waking up in a coldish room, in darkness, to a loud 'peep peep peep' every morning, just to frantically try to hit the snooze button - half-awake coming back from another (dream) planet is not my ideal wake-up call.

After advice from my good friend Henry, I got a Lumie wakeup light alarm. It simply lights up over the 30 minutes before your alarm is set, so by the time you're supposed to wake up, there is some light next to your bed. It can be quite bright and light up the room too, to make navigating around the room easier once you get up.

This was a game changer. After a few nights, I didn't even need the sound to wake up to the alarm, I was just waking up with the light. It felt way better, I was less confused and less grumpy in the mornings, which was a huge accomplishment and a step change. This in turn brought on other positive changes.

Setting a morning 'goal' or a reward
Before going to bed in the evening, or during the day, it's good to have a thing you want to do in the morning. It can be as simple as watching an educational video for 5 minutes, or doing a mini workout, anything that you wouldn't usually do in the morning. Something that adds a new meaning to waking up early. It can even be a reward like 15 minutes of playing games or whatever your guilty pleasure is, but you only get it if you wake up early and get up.

Getting things ready

I always leave my work space clean and organised enough, so that when I approach it in the morning it looks inviting. I want to make sure I don't have to clean any mess when I first wake up, as that's another negative block from getting productive and inspired.

If you want to go running, prep your gear. If you want to do yoga, prep your mat. If you want to meditate, prep your space and make it inviting, clutter-free.

Sleeping hacks to help you get more energy in the mornings

To have a truly great, awe-inspiring morning it is helpful to be awake and have some energy. The more energy we have in the morning, the more strength we have to complete a morning routine, boost this energy, grow it exponentially, and deposit it for the day.

Here are a few things that help me to fall asleep faster, sleep better, and recover better during sleep:

Use a blue screen filter

Always have a timed blue screen filter (I use flux) on your laptop and mobile phone in the evenings. I have them set to turn on from 8 pm every evening. Flux is great as you can set your levels and timers, and when you plug in your laptop into the TV, it transfers the effect onto the big screen.

My phone is also set to block out the blue in the evenings.

Meditate throughout the day

Every day I meditate during my morning routine, but then I try my best to do a tiny 5-10 minute relaxation after lunch and in the evening. This way I relax and 'stretch my brain' from daily stress and challenges. This ensures I don't build up tension there over the day and I'm not carrying around tons of unfinished business. I think this is what kept me awake at night in the past - having a lot of unfinished, stuck thoughts I didn't 'iron out' during the day, that wanted to realise themselves.

Don't eat 2-4 hours before bed

I try not to eat a few hours before sleeping. Living in Spain has been more challenging, as they have an evening-orientated lifestyle. For example, on the weekends all restaurants open at 7-8 pm, while I usually try to go to bed at 9.30 pm with the aim of falling asleep by 10. So occasionally I can't stick to this rule. Not only does eating late affect your sleep, but it also makes you store more fat from the food you ate. This isn't helpful if you're trying to lose weight or stay fit!

No caffeine after 3 pm

I drink a lot of coffee in the morning, I totally love it, especially if I have challenging projects on hand. I sometimes drink green tea after the coffee, to carry on the effects of it for longer. However, during the day, I aim to not have any caffeine after 3 pm, otherwise, it may keep me buzzing into the evening and make falling asleep harder. This includes all stimulants: no Coca-Cola, green tea, or energy drinks after 3 pm and into the evenings.

Get a well-shaped ergonomic pillow
Another breakthrough in my sleeping was from discovering a bad pillow really makes for a night of bad sleep. I used to use Zara Home pillows, then it was Ikea; as long as they're memory foam, or generally hard and mould to my neck, they're fine. With bad pillows, you may experience neck pain and wake up with more headaches due to it.

A mattress to suit your sleeping style
I'm still experimenting in this area. Usually I prefer memory foam mattresses, but the harder kind. They seem to be comfortable whether I sleep on my side, front or back. I recommend you experiment whenever possible. The easiest way to do this is to note how you slept in a given hotel, as they have different beds of varying hardness.

Have a 'breathing' cover
Whatever you use to cover yourself through the night should be as natural as possible and not create an impenetrable, non-breathable barrier. This results in sweating and lower comfort.

Make sure the room isn't too hot
That was another breakthrough! Sleeping in a cool room was way better for me than in a hot one. Especially while I lived in Asia - it was really hard to fall asleep without air conditioning, nearly impossible. It's also important to

make sure the room isn't freezing in the morning as that makes getting out of bed more challenging.

Making notes and planning the following day
Oftentimes we can't let go of the day and still have thoughts buzzing in our heads; there may be things we haven't accomplished during the day, that we wanted to do or things we worry about for the next day.

I make a lot of notes throughout the day, to take these ideas from my head, into another medium, to free up my mind from thinking I won't act on them.

I spend a lot of time throughout the day and evening planning the next day, before my 'cut off relaxing time'. I want to ensure that my mind is free of worry as I finish the working day.

Chapter 8
Mindsets and tips for daily performance

Turning on the explorer mode

When someone tells me about a new habit, lifestyle, or mindset they developed it's very easy to go straight to and emotional response and judge them from that viewpoint. It's almost automatic if we don't acknowledge it and stop it from happening.

If someone told you about a movie they saw and they say they enjoyed it, often even before they finish their sentence you scream 'What? This piece of stinking garbage, don't you have any taste in movies?' How different would the following conversation be if you simply asked: 'Why did you enjoy it?' or 'What did you find so good about it?' and then listened. Be open to the answers, who knows, maybe you missed a key plot, maybe they can't answer, but maybe there is something there you could've experienced and you haven't because you closed yourself off by jumping to judgement, rather than exploring.

By being explorers we can learn a lot more about anything.

The same applies to morning routines. If you stop judging them or the idea of building habits and instead explored and went deeper, you may find something amazing within.

One of the ways to learn to like something is to dive deeper into it and learn about it. Once you discover the depth of a field, the community around it, how beneficial it is to mankind - you appreciate it more and you're more likely to engage in it from a friendly, active, positive stance.

Limiting stress inputs through the day

We all know about information overload, but have you ever stopped and thought about your stress overload? About all the things you see, read, and hear that trigger a tiny pinch in your chest or stomach. Do they make you feel inadequate, scared, on the edge, or simply anxious?

That's potential stress input right there, that little pinch. Often social media is said to have that effect. But why is that? Maybe because we follow people who really annoy us, or post stuff that has no positive effect on us?

Why is reducing stressful inputs important?

Each negative/stressful input is like hostile noise; like trying to watch a show with all the interference, or listening to music while there are roadworks in the background.

Clarity brings us the best ideas and solutions.

Actions executed with clarity and presence bring the best results.

Take action today to reduce the stress you receive from the sources you can control.

Every day's a new opportunity

I used to have days when I would wake up and think to myself "Oh my god, not this again, all the responsibilities, the day job stress, the things I don't want to do, the pain in my back, my head is hurting, my muscles are sore". Whatever it is - I felt like every day I had to face it all again and survive that daily pain.

It took me years to figure out that it's actually the opposite - every day is a new opportunity to do things better, a literal 'Groundhog Day'. You can re-run and fix the things you missed the previous day

A promise you didn't keep.

A call you didn't make.

A client you didn't get.

A nice gesture for your partner you didn't do.

A better gym session (if you flaked out or skipped yesterday).

The hobby you didn't pursue.

The good habit you didn't keep.

Persistence in new initiatives, interests, and businesses

Josh Kaufman, the author of 'The First 20 Hours: Mastering the Toughest Part of Learning Anything' says it takes about 20 hours to get a grip on a new skill. I like that way more than what I heard previously... that it takes 10,000 hours!

I remember learning to swim more adequately as an adult and it definitely took longer than that! But once I got the hang of it, it was more enjoyable and I could proudly say I knew a bit about swimming. In no way was I great at it, but I could get into the water and not entirely embarrass myself, and felt confident in it. With time, this came to me feeling very natural in water and now I love swimming.

By embarking on a new interest, and realising how bad I am at it, I now remind myself it'll take at least 20 hours before I'm even a little bit OK at it.

Whatever your new initiative, business idea, or side hustle, give it some time before you decide you can't do it. Understand you'll naturally be bad at any new thing you undertake; persist and you'll see your skills grow with time and confidence! It also helps to maintain the attitude of not being scared of trying new things. It's a brilliant attitude to have!

It's easy to approach something, like the morning routine habit, and after trying it once or twice drop it and decide it doesn't work for you.

Try to run a marker sheet or put ticks in your notepad for every time you try something new and spend 30 minutes or an hour on it. Only consider giving up once you have dedicated 20 hours to it. Odds are that once you put in more hours over time, you will get better at a given activity and from that, joy will come to make you stick with it.

Evaluating your daily plans

Steve Jobs, from his commencement 2005 speech at Stanford: "for the past 33 years, I have looked in the mirror every morning and asked myself: '' if today were the last day of my life, would I want to do what I am about to do today?" And whenever the answer has been "No" for too many days in a row, I know I need to change something."[7]

What a brilliant example of keeping up with a morning planning routine, which no doubt contributed to Steve Jobs being one of the visionary leaders of our generation.

What a committed view to keep yourself accountable for making sure your life has meaning and delivers value.

Once I plan my day every morning, I ensure that I have

---

7   'You've got to find what you love,' Jobs says: https://news.stanford.edu/news/2005/june15/jobs-061505.html

some things there for my body, mind, spirituality, family, and business. That every main area of my life is getting some of my attention.

The portion of attention always shifts, every day, depending on where I'm falling short.

Say I've been working very hard for a few days and haven't spent any time with my partner, I should probably do something nice for her to make up for it and show her she does matter, it's just that I had urgent business priorities that will provide for us and our future.

Alternatively, maybe I neglected exercising for a few days. I should probably then add more exercise and put notes in my online calendar for the weekend, to ensure that I make up for any lack of activity during the week.

Once you're done with planning your day in the morning and are ready to head 'into the real world' and face it, it is advisable to evaluate the plan and ask if it feels like today's list will:

1. Make a real change for the better in your life circumstance.

2. Help you be a better person.

3. Deliver value to those around you.

4. At the end of the day, upon completion, make you feel like you progressed today.

Building on the small habits and small wins

"In the shapeliness of a life, habit plays its sovereign role... Most people take action by habit in small things more often than in important things, for it's the simple matters that get done readily, while the more sombre and interesting, taking more effort and being more complex, often must wait for another day. Thus, we could improve ourselves quite well by habit, by its judicious assistance, but it's more likely that habits rule us." - **Mary Oliver** [8]

Habits make up the majority of our lives and seem to rule most of our decisions. If you're a smoker you don't consciously think before picking up that cigarette, it's automatic at certain parts of the day or when things get stressful. Do you really control your life fully if you snack away at popcorn? Have you ever tried to just eat 1/10th of a pack of crisps or just drink ⅓ of a can of fizzy drink? These troublesome habits are really hard to stop midway because we do them almost mindlessly.

If the small habits rule our lives and we do them without thinking, automatically, surely it would make sense to grow

8 Long life : essays and other writings: http://www.worldcat.org/title/long-life-essays-and-other-writings/oclc/53951016&referer=brief_results

more positive ones? Once you replace the sugar from a candy bar with a banana, and you do this consistently, soon enough, without engaging any willpower, you're eating healthier.

The same logic applies to swapping fizzy drinks for water, homemade lemonade, or tea. Eventually, once you've learned that habit it'll become effortless.

Once you make a habit of getting some small wins in the morning, start to sprinkle them around. Have a small win after lunch so if you're feeling a bit slow after eating, you can 'pick yourself up' naturally with an easy win.

It's just playing this daily game of scheduling strategically. Don't just throw things at your to-do list and in your calendar willy-nilly. Consider the day ahead, how you may feel, your energy levels, how the events of the day may impact you, and be prepared.

Do one thing at a time or bind activities in pairs

Our brains don't particularly like to multitask - this shouldn't be news to anyone, jumping from one mind intensive activity to another breaks the flow.

During habits performance, a similar rule applies where, if you're performing one learned habit, it's better to completely finish it before proceeding to the next one:

"The interneurons were activated during the time when

the rats were in the middle of performing the learned sequence, and could possibly be preventing the principal neurons from initiating another routine until the current one was finished. The discovery of this opposite activity by the interneurons also gets us one step closer to understanding how brain circuits can actually produce this pattern of activity," Martiros says. (source: Massachusetts Institute of Technology. "Distinctive brain pattern helps habits form: Study identifies neurons that fire at the beginning and end of a behaviour as it becomes a habit."[9]

I won't start the next stage of my morning routine before the first one is completed, but I do combine some elements.

So, for example, I will watch a motivational video while making coffee.

Or I will exercise while watching 'awe-inspiring' videos.

I will sometimes work on the more mundane tasks while listening to great thinkers like Jordan Peterson or Sam Harris.

They don't conflict with each other; I'd even say they support one another. The talks from the great minds of our world support my creative thinking and often help me find a better solution to the problems I'm facing.

The 'awe-inspiring' videos motivate me to go harder while exercising or stretching, doing activities more mindfully and going deeper into my muscles to actively relax them.

---

9   ScienceDaily,   8   February   2018   www.sciencedaily.com/releases/
    2018/02/180208120923.htm

Turning mornings into a hobby

Turn mornings into hobbies; add little elements, think about how they could be even better, experiment with the coffee or tea you drink, have something different to eat on different days, reward yourself for the experience.

A brilliant way to make yourself stick to morning routines is to continuously fine-tune them. So research other people's routines and what the most successful people do and experiment with it, play with it. One week try waking up 30 minutes earlier and add an extra element. Next week wake up 15 minutes later and remove one activity. Always continue to learn and improve your morning routine as it can always be better.

Doing things in a group is always preferable and if you can find people who also wake up around the same time, share your morning routine with them and find out about theirs. People may always be doing something different to you, that could be beneficial to you.

Chapter 9

Normal or mediocre is not good enough anymore

'Comfort is the enemy of progress.' -
P.T. Barnum.

We live in a time of the biggest technological break-throughs humanity has ever witnessed. Daily we read about new scientific discoveries that could change how the world operates. We often hear about another illness cured and removed from our future worries; just look at how the management of diabetes has evolved over the last 20 years, and it's still moving at a great pace.

In these times of ultimate opportunity, more equality in our societies than ever, and fewer wars than ever, we can become a bit stagnant and feel too comfortable.

And as we know 'comfort is the enemy of progress' (P.T. Barnum).

It's through rising to challenges that we grow and improve; if we constantly steer away from pain and difficulty, back towards the feeling of being in our mother's womb, we won't grow. That's also how mediocre lives are built, by staying comfortable as much as possible, not risking, not growing, not exposing yourself to possible failure, from which you could learn.

I'm not a huge fan of failing, yet I can't help but look at my past and see the failures as really important lessons in my life and now that I see them from a distance it's clear to me how they've contributed to my current state and where I am in life.

At the time of failing, or not being able to step up to challenges, I couldn't see how they were contributing positively to my life. I was shouting out 'make it stop, this is too hard' when my mind and body were actually learning and improving.

I think the quote "Fail early, fail often, but always fail forward." by John C. Maxwell is very true, but too many start-ups are just playing with other people's money and not always 'failing forward'. We can't afford to fail all the time in our lives. Tell someone raising their child to start playing fast and loose with their upbringing or college fund and I don't think they'll be inspired and compliant, in fact, they may laugh at you.

However, the truth is that we should keep trying, aim to do things better, try new solutions and experiment, within reason, with our approaches. If you do the same thing, the same way, the outcome will likely be the same.

In our society being average is no longer a means to survival. There is no job security, robots are taking over the basic jobs. Who knows what else they'll take over in the future and when this will happen. If you're just average or 'good enough' at your job, odds are that in a few years either someone will be hired to replace you, above you or, due to company issues, you may be let go from your post.

Our only security is in constantly improving, bringing innovation, and presenting the best you whenever possible. If you're always improving and growing as a person then no matter what life throws at you, you're more likely to have the tools and mindset to handle it.

Having a good morning routine and trying to mimic the most successful people on this planet (most of whom do have a morning routine) should be a priority for your future wellbeing.

Chapter 10

Modern morning routines to help you build yours

Anastasiia - digital nomad, teacher, subtitles specialist

My morning routine is easy, at least in theory. Three main things I want to accomplish every morning before 10am are: to wake up my mind, to wake up my muscles and to wake up my digestive system.

I usually wake up at 7:45. Let's start with the mind - yes I do start with my phone first thing in the morning. Even if you can't resist using your phone straight away, make it useful - my suggestions are either an audiobook (something educational or thought provoking) or your favourite music (FYI: classical music works. Even if you're not a big Mozart/Bach-fan just give it a shot, you may be surprised).

Then with headphones in my ears, I'm off to the bathroom - brush teeth, wash face - you know the drill. I usually do at least 5 min. of face-gymnastic/massage - and this is how you start your blood moving faster. It can be quite entertaining in front of the mirror and with the music in your ears, add some hopping to this and you will start your day with an ironic smile or even a proper giggle, what can be better?

Then I relocate myself to the kitchen, yes I'm making breakfast for us.

I usually start with a cup of coffee and try to keep the breakfasts healthy and nutritious. Our breakfasts are usually spiced with meaningful conversations about the upcoming day or about interesting things which we've read, heard or thought about (we are kinda dorks - so this part is really optional, just find your topics or something brain engaging to do while eating, or just eat mindfully!)

After breakfast most days I do my yoga + meditation session.

The most important thing is the plan, you should know what you do, don't wake up into the unknown or into "I'll see how it goes". Leave the improvisations to the second part of your day. And yes explain to the ones you live with that this is how you function the best and you know what you're doing.

Bruce Cat - Entrepreneur, startups investor.

Most people would try to copy someone else's morning routine, simply because they think that if they copy a successful habit they too will be successful. That's simply a wrong way of doing things. A morning routine is personal. It depends on where you're at in life and what is your main focus and goals.

My morning routine today is not the same as it was 5 years ago, 2 years ago or even a year ago as my goals are not the same as back then. Don't copy someone's ending, copy where they were when they were at your level.

5 years ago, my goal was to make millions and speed and time were everything to me. My morning routines would look something like this. Wake up at 6am, drink warm water, meditate for an hour, eat breakfast (usually smoothies followed by bitter coffee.) Because my working day started the night before, by scheduling my day before I got to bed, I'd have plenty of time in the morning.

Nowadays, I have made my free time a priority by appointing CEOs for every company. Life is not meant for being a slave to work. Most people are slaves, but they don't know that they are slaves.

I wake up at 8am. Do 15 mins of stretching, followed by some reading. I then do 20 minutes of water wheel meditation, 1 hour of standing meditation, 30 minutes of chi gong, then end the morning with some stretching. After that it's breakfast. I do this routine 3x a day.

Chokae Kalekoa - Yoga and meditation instructor, life coach and my mentor for over 10 years now.

My morning routine begins at the moment I am conscious, before I even get out of bed. After many years of practice, it is now quite natural for me to wake up and do a few repetitions of pranayama techniques as various chants or mantras reveal themselves in the foreground of my consciousness - when I'm fully awake, I tend to go directly into a simple meditation sesh, stretching a bit, then sitting up in a simple posture on the bed - from there pretty much anything can happen! However, regardless of what's next on my agenda, I am always confident that I've checked in with myself inside and out before moving on to my morning ablutions and breakfast.

John Doherty - Founder & CEO at Credo

Over the years as an entrepreneur I've become a big fan of morning routines. Before my daughter was born in April 2019, I had a very set routine where I would wake up around 6am, make coffee, write in my Five Minute Journal, and get into work for two hours before eating, showering, and getting back into work for the day.

Since my daughter was born my routine has changed and often gets interrupted (plus, I am more tired), but I make time every day for my Five Minute Journal because I find that beginning my day with gratitude and the three major things to accomplish that day keeps me focused and helps reduce anxiety and feelings of not accomplishing enough. Once I get my three big tasks for the day done, the rest of the day is a bonus.

**Harriet Green, CEO and Chairman,
IBM Asia Pacific**

"Up around 3.30, work on emails and actions to prep the day from around the world. 4.30 to 5.30 run, tennis, gym, my time! At my desk by 6.30/7 ready to dive into our teams, clients or partners."

Chapter 11
Sticking with it

Keeping your morning routine habit

Like with any habit, the key part is sticking to it, despite your mind sometimes not wanting to continue with the routine.

As below research states, some people may be 'habit-resistant' - previously we believed it only takes 21 days to form a habit, the latest research suggests it's actually more like 66 days, and for some even more.

Take it one day at a time instead and don't worry whether it'll take you a week or two months to form a strong habit. Just focus on doing your morning routine, even if you wake up late, even if unexpected events occur, even if you reduce your morning to a minimum of three steps, but still get it in.

Don't worry about trying to do this every single day, as missing a day will not reduce the chances of forming a habit. But don't make a habit out of missing habits, if you catch my drift.

John M. Grohol, Psy.D. states in his article:

"Although the average was 66 days, there was marked variation in how long habits took to form, anywhere from 18 days up to 254 days in the habits examined in this study. As you'd imagine, drinking a daily glass of water becomes automatic very quickly but doing 50 sit-ups before breakfast required more dedication (above, dotted lines). The researchers also noted that:

- Missing a single day did not reduce the chance of forming a habit.

- A sub-group took much longer than the others to form their habits, perhaps suggesting some people are 'habit-resistant'.

- Other types of habits may well take much longer."[10]

Lone wolf? Still better off in a wolf pack.

I always considered myself to be an individual; when I was younger, perhaps I felt as though I didn't fully fitted in.

Growing up, I always felt a drive towards values or activities different from those of my peer group. I was more of an introvert - books, role-playing, and PC games were the daily bread and butter of what I spent my time on.

During this period, I was always striving for some goal or

10 Need to Form a New Habit? Give Yourself At Least 66 Days: https://psychcentral.com/blog/need-to-form-a-new-habit-66-days/

unattainable star on the horizon. This made me feel that I was a lone wolf, independent of my family, friends, or partners and that I could do everything on my own.

How wrong was I? Since I joined the Journey 2 Greatness (our self-improvement project) with my friends and once we started sharing daily goals and logging our meditation on WhatsApp, I became a different being.

My performance skyrocketed because now I was accountable.

I find that when I share with others something I'm working on or a hobby I'm pursuing, it helps me to keep motivated and cracking on despite setbacks.

If I feel like giving up, say, morning running, I imagine myself telling everyone that I had told that I was running, why I stopped - and through this, I can see how silly that would sound and what silly excuse I would invent. Then I just carry on, because I know that the opinion of my friends matters to me, it incentivises me to keep going. I'd much prefer to share with everyone how I have run for yet another morning, than admitting I gave up a habit that I was raving about last week.

A great way to achieve responsibility-sharing is to set up an accountability group. As part of the resources on the previous page, I mention a few groups you may want to join, to help you keep up the habit of morning routines and waking up at a set time.

If you can do this with your partner, that's great - this way you have your accountability partner right there. If there's no one in your household, no problem, just do it over the internet and find people to team up with as accountability buddies. Ideally they should be in the same time zone and wake up at a similar time to you.

An exercise to help you stay accountable

It is a fact that staying accountable helps build habits. David Goggins, in his book 'Can't Hurt Me: Master Your Mind and Defy the Odds', had a great exercise to get people in the right frame of mind. I thought it was a great idea as nothing builds accountability into your day like a bit of peer pressure.

I've posted in a WhatsApp groups every single day, for years now. If I'm struggling with a task I'll share it with our group and ask to be kept accountable. They then message or call me by the end of the day to check if I finished the task if I haven't posted.

Often I share my weekly tasks with my partner. She then helps me stay accountable and I know, if I go to her at the end of the week and say 'Honey, I just didn't have the time' - she knows better and she knows I had the time, she won't take any excuses, so I just go and do the thing I said I'd do. This in turn makes following through on life easier.

If you want to start your morning routine from Monday,

then on Monday post on your social media with the hashtag #aweinspiringmornings.

You can post a photo of your morning routine or write it up, I don't mind, whatever works for you. Make sure to post 'This is my morning routine', so any time you want to give up or start making excuses (as we all do sometimes), you can remind yourself 'Oh wait I told everyone I'll be doing this, I can't just stop now'.

The Monday message should include a promise that you will carry on, this way you make yourself accountable. Keep this promise to yourself! This way you reaffirm and show others you're on a journey and put yourself under a little bit of pressure which will help you not to give up on this new habit.

Keeping up your motivation to stick to morning routines

"People often say that motivation doesn't last. Well, neither does bathing—that's why we recommend it daily" - **Zig Ziglar**

Many things don't last in life, many activities must be performed daily to maintain our lifestyle and quality of life. Think brushing your teeth, making your bed, doing the dishes, you get the idea.

You can't say in life 'I'm successful so I'm done with

working on my success' - this is how stagnation starts, and a slow fall. I don't necessarily follow the age-old rule of "When you stop growing you start dying." by William S. Burroughs. I think it's often natural to stay at a given level, it's when you let things slip and deteriorate that you're truly losing out.

We can't ever be 'done' with keeping fit or eating healthy. That would result in us being unhealthy in the long term, to a considerable degree. Just like we can't ever be 'done' with breathing, or being part of society.

Even with relationships, once you settle down and you think you're 'done' with relationships , maybe you're even married, no - the game has only just started, it has just changed now. Now, the aim isn't to find a partner or get as many girls' numbers as you can in one night, none of that silliness, now the aim is to make this other person's life as wonderful as possible to continue providing value.

Once you learn to read, you aren't done with books. Just because you learned a skill, doesn't mean you're 'done' in that field. You're only now entering the real game, the game of studying, learning, and gaining new skills and knowledge from books, that were not accessible to you in the past.

The same goes for awe-inspiring morning routines. Now that you've discovered the power behind them, it's up to you to continue improving them, maintaining the habit, sharing the huge potential they bring to life with your loved ones. It's true that as a single person we can't change the world for the better, but if we spread the good practices, share the joy, and help others, this energy multiplies and leads to first local change, neighbourhood change, and then (through the wonders of social media) global change.

So please don't think of this progress and process as solely your own journey. By doing the right things and radiating energy outwards, we are changing the world for the better. Ultimately, that's what I hope this book will help do, in some tiny capacity. Thank you for being part of this journey!

Printed in Great Britain
by Amazon